Original title:
Frosted Skies

Copyright © 2024 Swan Charm
All rights reserved.

Author: Kaido Väinamäe
ISBN HARDBACK: 978-9916-79-543-9
ISBN PAPERBACK: 978-9916-79-544-6
ISBN EBOOK: 978-9916-79-545-3

Patterns of Stillness in an Icy World

In the hush of the night sky,
Stars blink like secrets shared,
Whispers dance on frosty breath,
Nature's canvas softly prepared.

Silhouettes of trees stand tall,
Cloaked in shimmering white,
Branches bow with heavy peace,
In the heart of winter's night.

Moonlight sketches shadows long,
Over fields of untouched snow,
Each flake tells a quiet tale,
Where gentle breezes flow.

Footprints print a fleeting path,
Leading to a world serene,
Every step a story told,
In a realm where dreams convene.

Silent echoes cradle time,
A stillness wraps the land,
Within the icy tapestry,
Life pauses at nature's hand.

Ethereal Romance in Coldness

Beneath the frosty moonlight glow,
Two hearts entwined, feeling the flow.
In the silence, whispers ignite,
Love blooms softly in the cold night.

Snowflakes fall like gentle sighs,
Veiling secrets beneath the skies.
Hand in hand, we embrace the chill,
In this stillness, time stands still.

Whispers of Winter's Veil

The world adorned in blankets white,
Each breath a fog in the soft twilight.
As shadows dance on icy ground,
Winter's whispers, a sweet sound.

The trees stand tall, their limbs embrace,
Holding memories in this space.
Footprints left, a trace of you,
In this realm where dreams come true.

Shimmering Celestial Blanket

Underneath the starry dome,
We wander through the starlit foam.
Each twinkle tells a story grand,
In the night, together we stand.

Frost-kissed air, a soothing balm,
In your warmth, the world is calm.
With every glance, galaxies swirl,
In this dance, our hearts unfurl.

Icy Breath at Dusk

As day surrenders to the night,
Chill lingers in the fading light.
Breath of winter, crisp and pure,
In this moment, love is sure.

Footsteps echo in the hush,
At dusk, all around, the rush.
Wrapped in warmth, a tender bliss,
Time stands still in an icy kiss.

Dreamlit Ice-flecked Expanse

Across the frozen land, so wide,
Dreams shimmer under a crystal tide.
Stars twinkle in the moonlit veil,
Silent whispers in the frosty gale.

Winds weave tales of ancient lore,
Carving secrets to the core.
The night dances with soft delight,
Awakening spirits in the frosty night.

Each breath a mist, each step a song,
In this expanse where we belong.
Underneath the vast, dark sky,
Hope ignites as the dreams fly high.

Ice-flecked shadows gently move,
Guided by the heart's own groove.
Nature's canvas, pure and bright,
Paints the world in silver light.

With every dawn, the chill recedes,
Awakening the life's hidden seeds.
Beneath the surface, warmth will rise,
In the dreamlit land beneath the skies.

Night's Lullaby in Glacial Light

In twilight's grasp, the world stands still,
A lullaby whispers over the hill.
The moon, a guardian, watches near,
Calming the hearts, dispelling fear.

Icicles shimmer, a delicate sight,
Casting reflections in the pale night.
The stars join in, twinkling soft,
As the night's lullaby begins to waft.

Frosted branches sway with grace,
Nature's beauty in this serene place.
Each note a promise, sweet and low,
In glacial light, the dreams will flow.

Embracing shadows, we close our eyes,
Under the cloak of vast, dark skies.
A world transformed by silver's charm,
In night's embrace, we find our calm.

With dawn's first glow, the song will fade,
Yet in our hearts, the memories stayed.
Resonating softly, like a gentle breeze,
Night's lullaby brings the soul to ease.

Traces of Frost in Radiant Afterglow

The sun retreats, embracing the night,
Leaving remnants of day, a fading light.
Frosted whispers paint the ground,
In radiant afterglow, peace is found.

Morning's chill wraps the earth with grace,
Traces of frost in a delicate lace.
The world awakens, fresh and bright,
As shadows dance with the coming light.

Underneath the trees, a blanket lies,
Glistening jewels, like tears from the skies.
Each breath we take, a frosty delight,
In the tapestry woven by nature's sight.

Amidst the glow of the setting sun,
The day's journey is almost done.
Fleeting moments, like snowflakes fall,
Radiant memories weave through it all.

As twilight lingers, the magic grows,
In traces of frost, the heart knows.
Embracing the night, we find our way,
In the splendor of dusk, we choose to stay.

Celestial Ice and Twilight's Embrace

In twilight's heart, a world unfolds,
Celestial ice in stories told.
Stars emerge from hiding spots,
Casting light on forgotten thoughts.

Frosty breath upon the air,
Nature whispers, a secret stare.
Every shadow holds a tale,
Of winter winds that softly wail.

In the embrace of a chilly night,
Dreams take flight, glowing bright.
Sparkling crystals, a dazzling sight,
Celestial wonders fill the night.

With each heartbeat, the universe sings,
As stars twinkle, the magic brings.
Under a sky where dreams align,
In twilight's embrace, our spirits shine.

Endless horizons stretch so wide,
In the dance of ice, love will abide.
Bound by the night's gentle grace,
We find solace in this sacred space.

Starlit Whispers on a Frosty Canvas

Beneath the stars, the night is still,
A world covered in whispers, a gentle thrill.
Frost paints the trees, a sparkling lace,
In this quiet moment, we find our place.

Moonlight dances on the frosty ground,
Echoes of silence, a beauty profound.
Each breath a cloud, softly we see,
As starlit secrets embrace you and me.

A Glint of Ice Above the Earth

Crystals shimmer in the pale moonlight,
A glint of ice, a breathtaking sight.
Branches adorned with nature's grace,
Reflecting the calm of this sacred space.

The world is bound in a frosty dream,
Where everything sparkles and begins to gleam.
Underneath the stars, hope takes flight,
In the chill of the hour, hearts burn bright.

Tranquility Wrapped in Crystal Light

Whispers of frost in the morning air,
Nature's embrace, an answer to prayer.
Sunrise breaks through, painting the scenes,
A canvas of white, where nothing intervenes.

Each flake a jewel, unique in form,
Creating a hush, as if to warn.
In tranquility, we find our peace,
Wrapped in the crystal, we find release.

Gleaming Horizons of a Silent Night

Horizons aglow, the sky deep and wide,
Gleaming and quiet, where dreams reside.
Stars like lanterns, glowing so bright,
Guiding our hearts through the silent night.

A world hushed and soft, wrapped in embrace,
In the stillness found, we discover our place.
With whispers of night, we journey anew,
Under starlit skies, our spirits break through.

Dreams Cradled in Cold Ambiance

In the stillness of night's embrace,
Whispers of dreams drift through space.
Snowflakes descend with delicate grace,
Carrying wishes in their soft lace.

A blanket of white, silent and deep,
Holds the secrets that winter keeps.
In slumber, the world is lulled to sleep,
As visions of warmth in hearts do leap.

The stars above twinkle with care,
Guiding lost souls through chilled air.
Each breath released as a frosty flare,
Painting hope in the night so rare.

Within the silence, hearts find peace,
From burdens of life, they seek release.
In dreams cradled, fears will cease,
A tranquil moment, a sweet increase.

So let the cold wrap you tight,
As dreams bloom softly in the night.
With every breath, find your light,
In the ambiance, hold on to what feels right.

Signs of the Wintry Breath

With every gust, the whisper starts,
A tale of winter in chilly parts.
Trees stand bare, like old, worn arts,
Scribbled stories of nature's hearts.

Specks of frost on window panes,
Nature's artistry in silver chains.
A canvas painted with icy stains,
The wintry breath breaks all the lanes.

Footprints crunch on layers white,
Echoing softly through the night.
In the quiet, dreams ignite,
Under stars that sparkle bright.

Hooded figures glide with ease,
In a world wrapped in winter's freeze.
Each breath suspended, whispers tease,
As swirling winds through branches tease.

The season's chill brings a sigh,
Yet warms the heart like a soft reply.
In each silence, we learn to fly,
Embracing dreams as we pass by.

The Light Dance of Chill

Frost captures the morning light,
A crystal ballet, pure and bright.
Each shimmer gives the day a bite,
As shadows flee with fading night.

Lose yourself in the frosty air,
Where laughter rings and spirits share.
Children twirl without a care,
In a wonderland forever fair.

Beneath the trees, the snowflakes glide,
As whispers of cold attempt to hide.
The world will spin, and dreams abide,
In the chill, hearts open wide.

Through icy breezes, the branches sway,
Dancing with joy in a frosty play.
Nature invites us, come what may,
In the chill light, we'll find our way.

The day transforms as shadows lengthen,
In the twilight glow, new dreams strengthen.
Allow the chill to be your beacon,
In the light dance, find your reason.

Hushed Hues of Frost's Touch

In the quietude of winter's sway,
Colors fade in a muted display.
Pastels merge with the clouds of gray,
Hushed hues that softly drift away.

Each petal crowned with shimmering frost,
Bears the weight of beauty, never lost.
In silence, the world counts the cost,
Of fleeting moments that are embossed.

Branches wrapped in glittering white,
Whisper tales of the silent night.
Underneath the cover, hearts take flight,
Awakening dreams in gentle light.

With each breath, the chill is found,
In layers thick, nature's sound.
Embrace the stillness that surrounds,
For in the hush, true beauty abounds.

Through frosty lenses, we see anew,
A world reborn in delicate hue.
In winter's hold, our spirits grew,
As hush descends on a canvas of blue.

Dappled Light on Crisp Clouds

Sunlight pierces through the veil,
Casting shadows, soft and pale.
Whispers of a gentle breeze,
Rustling through the autumn trees.

Golden hues that dance and sway,
Painting skies at close of day.
Clouds adorned with flecks of gold,
Stories of the day retold.

Nature's palette, vibrant and bright,
Blends the day into the night.
Dreams aloft on air's embrace,
Finding comfort in this space.

Colors fade but memories stay,
In the twilight's gentle play.
A moment caught in fleeting light,
As day yields to the night.

So breathe in deep this fleeting scene,
Where daylight lingers in between.
The peace that only skies can bring,
Resonates, as night takes wing.

Chilled Serenades of the Heavens

Whispers echo in the cool,
Amidst the stars, a silent rule.
Moonlight dances on the frost,
Beauty found, though warmth is lost.

Notes of night in harmony,
Resonate with clarity.
Each breath a puff of icy air,
Filling hearts with quiet care.

Crickets hum their lullabies,
As constellations fill the skies.
A symphony of winter's grace,
In every shadow, space, and place.

The night unfolds, a canvas deep,
Where dreams awaken from their sleep.
Every twinkle tells a tale,
Of hope, of loss, of love's fair trail.

In this realm of chilly air,
Serenades whisper, gently share.
Underneath the cosmos wide,
We find comfort, side by side.

Morning's Frosty Ballet

In the dawn, the world awakes,
With frosty breath that gently shakes.
Sunrise pierces through the chill,
Painting skies with winter's thrill.

Pine trees clutch their icy crowns,
As daylight sweeps away the frowns.
Footsteps crunch on silent ground,
Each moment new, fresh joy is found.

Bare branches stretch towards the sun,
In elegant dance, they twirl and run.
Frosted mirrors twinkle bright,
Reflecting warmth from morning light.

Birdsong fills the crisp, cool air,
A serenade beyond compare.
Nature's stage in pure ballet,
As night bows out, and morn holds sway.

With every breath, the day unfolds,
A tapestry of gems and golds.
In winter's arms, we find our grace,
In morning's frosty, sweet embrace.

Celestial Crystals at Dusk

As daylight fades and shadows creep,
The heavens stir from their deep sleep.
Stars awaken, twinkling bright,
In a tapestry of cosmic light.

Each crystal glimmers, catches sight,
Dancing through the velvet night.
Stories whispered on the breeze,
Carried softly through the trees.

Constellations weave their threads,
Spinning dreams where starlight spreads.
Galaxies pulse in rhythmic flow,
The universe begins to glow.

Moonlight spills like silver dew,
Wrapping earth in an ethereal hue.
In the stillness, hearts take flight,
Guided gently by the night.

A cosmic quilt upon our skin,
Promises of journeys to begin.
In celestial realms, we find our place,
Among the stars, a warm embrace.

The Slice of Time in an Icy Dome

In a crystal world, the moments freeze,
Caught in whispers of a chilling breeze.
Echoes linger in the silent night,
Time suspended in the soft moonlight.

Each breath a fog, a fleeting thought,
In icy echoes, dreams are caught.
Reflections shimmer with a frosty glow,
A slice of time that flows so slow.

Wonders hidden in the glacial frame,
Shadows dance without a name.
Facets sparkle in the darkened sky,
Where whispers of the past slip by.

Glacial stories etched in white,
Stories told in the stillness of light.
The dome encases all that we find,
A tapestry that binds heart and mind.

Moments melt like snowflakes fall,
As silence answers winter's call.
In this frozen expanse we stay,
Alive in the night, lost in the day.

A Dance of Light on Frosted Veils

Beneath the moon's soft, silvery touch,
Frosted veils gleam, not asking much.
Each shimmer sways in the evening chill,
A dance of light, a surreal thrill.

Whispers glide through the icy air,
A ballet of shadows, delicate and rare.
Twirling softly with the stars above,
Embracing the moment, as if in love.

Glistening glades reflect the night,
Where every step brings a new delight.
In this realm where dreams unfold,
The frosty veils, a dance of gold.

Every flicker, a story's grace,
Tracing paths in an endless space.
The cool embrace of winter's song,
Draws us closer, where we belong.

In the quiet, we journey far,
Guided gently by each twinkling star.
Lost in this world, we find our way,
As the dance of light holds sway.

The Lure of a Frosty Horizon

Beyond the hills, the frosty edge,
Awaits a call, a whispered pledge.
Where winter's breath meets the morning light,
The horizon glimmers, sharp and bright.

Blades of grass, dressed in white,
Stand like soldiers in the fading night.
Each glinting frost, a world untold,
The lure of beauty, a sight to behold.

Footprints scatter across the field,
As nature's wonders slowly yield.
The promise of warmth in the gathering dawn,
Where icy dreams and sunlight spawn.

A tapestry woven with hope anew,
Every breath a melody, pure and true.
The frosty horizon, a beckoning trance,
Entices the heart to dream and dance.

In this place where the cold winds sigh,
We chase the gleam of the azure sky.
Forever drawn to the shimmering line,
The lure remains, eternally divine.

Embraced by Luminescence and Chill

Under the stars, a world so bright,
Embraced by warmth, yet kissed by night.
Luminescence dances on icy streams,
Where shadows whisper and silence dreams.

Crystals form where the moonlight falls,
A symphony echoes through hushed halls.
Each flicker a secret, a tale to tell,
Of a heart that beats where wonders dwell.

In the embrace of the chilly air,
We find a solace, a moment rare.
Together with stars, we weave a spell,
Lost in the depths where magic dwells.

Gardens of frost cradle the night,
As we wander under soft, pale light.
Each breath a story, each step a chance,
In the dance of life, we twirl and prance.

So let us bask in this mystical glow,
A world of secrets that softly flow.
With luminescence wrapped in a chill,
We find our peace, our hearts can fill.

Veils of Ice and Starry Night

Under the veil of twilight's grace,
Stars twinkle in a frozen space.
Cold winds whisper, secrets unfold,
Dreams wrapped in the night's bold hold.

Moonlight kisses the icy ground,
In the silence, a soft sound.
Shadows dance on frosted trees,
Nature breathes in the chilly breeze.

Glistening crystals twine and weave,
In every heart, the night shall cleave.
A tapestry of silver hue,
Painting dreams in skies of blue.

The night wears her icy crown,
Veiled in frost, she wanders down.
A journey crafted in quiet flight,
Amidst the veils of ice and night.

As dawn approaches, a gentle sigh,
The frozen veil begins to lie.
Yet in the heart, the stars remain,
Veils of ice, a sweet refrain.

Celestial Paint on an Icy Canvas

A canvas framed in twilight's glow,
Brushstrokes of chill, a cosmic show.
Stars dip low, in colors bright,
Painting dreams in the tranquil night.

Each flake of snow, an artist's hand,
Cascading down like grains of sand.
Layer by layer, the picture grows,
Celestial tales in winter's prose.

A palette rich with hues of blue,
In the silence, a world anew.
Crimson dawn on blankets white,
Whispers linger in morning light.

Above the frost, the heavens swirl,
A dance of light, a cosmic whirl.
In every twinkle, stories told,
Celestial dreams in the night unfold.

On this canvas, love is cast,
Moments captured, memories vast.
An artwork forged in starry night,
Celestial paint, a pure delight.

Echoes of Winter's Glimmer

Hushed whispers weave through icy air,
Winter's glimmer, a magical flair.
Echoes of silence, soft and clear,
Dancing in shadows, so near, so dear.

Frosty breath on the morning pane,
Every sparkle, a gentle rain.
Footsteps crunch on the frozen ground,
In winter's grip, a lullaby sound.

Shimmering light on the silver trees,
Nature bows with grace and ease.
A symphony of hidden sights,
Echoes of joy in starry nights.

With every glance, the heart shall swoon,
Under the watch of the glowing moon.
Fleeting moments, memories chime,
Winter's glimmer, a dance with time.

In the stillness, magic brews,
Painting the world in radiant views.
Echoes linger through the night air,
A symphony of winter's care.

The Quiet Dance of Snowy Nimbus

In the hush of dusk, the snowflakes twine,
A quiet dance, serene and fine.
Nimbus clouds in soft embrace,
Whirling down in gentle grace.

A whisper floats on the chilly breeze,
Bringing peace among the trees.
Each flake a heart that longs to share,
A moment caught in winter's snare.

Footprints trace along the white,
A map of love in frosty light.
Lost in the beauty of this trance,
In the quiet, we find our chance.

With every drift, the earth transformed,
A world reborn, silence warmed.
In stillness, the snowy nimbus sways,
A gentle rhythm in winter's play.

So let us dance in this quiet night,
Under the glow of the soft moonlight.
In every swirl, a dream shall rise,
The snowy nimbus, where magic lies.

A Tangle of Crystal Dreams

In a forest where whispers glide,
Beneath branches wide and proud,
Crystal dreams are trapped inside,
Sparkling softly, like a shroud.

Moonlight dances on the stream,
Casting shadows in the night,
Every flutter feels like a dream,
Wrapping the world in silver light.

Leaves shimmer with a transient grace,
Echoes of laughter float in the air,
In this enchanted, timeless place,
Hearts weave magic everywhere.

Threads of starlight knit the sky,
Woven secrets, old and new,
As the gentle moments sigh,
The world drifts, embraced by blue.

Every heartbeat, a whisper near,
A tapestry of hope and fears,
In this realm where dreams appear,
Fleeting moments turn to years.

Frozen Reverie in Shades of Gray

In the quiet, a stillness reigns,
The world draped in muted tones,
Every breath leaves frosty chains,
Where silence echoes, winter moans.

Shades of gray paint the landscape,
Blanketing memories so stark,
Each branch a fragile, frosted drape,
The sun's light dances, a timid spark.

Reflections wait in icy pools,
Softly capturing a dream's flight,
Whispers carried by nature's rules,
Breath of winter, a tender night.

As dusk falls, shadows intertwine,
Each moment wrapped in twilight's fold,
With flickering stars that brightly shine,
Tales of warmth in a chill so bold.

In this frozen reverie, I dwell,
Lost in the gray, a serene maze,
Where time moves slowly, casting a spell,
In dreams that flicker through winter's haze.

Lullabies of the Winter Air

Gentle whispers through the night,
Lullabies on a silver breeze,
Cradled softly in starlit light,
A serenade among the trees.

Snowflakes dance like tender dreams,
Filling the silence with their grace,
Nature's song unfolds in streams,
As night wraps its warm embrace.

Every flake a story told,
While shadows play on the ground,
In the stillness, the world feels bold,
A symphony that knows no sound.

Through the dark, a gentle glow,
Hints of warmth beneath the chill,
As hopes awaken, softly flow,
Easing hearts, a tranquil thrill.

In this winter night so rare,
Lullabies weave dreams with care,
A tender peace we all can share,
Wrapped in love, the world laid bare.

Arctic Serenade of the Twilight

In twilight's grasp, the cold winds sigh,
The arctic air, a crisp embrace,
As colors blend in the fading sky,
Nature's beauty finds its place.

Icebergs gleam like distant stars,
Their reflections dance on the sea,
While the horizon shimmers far,
Crafting dreams that yearn to be.

Whales sing songs that pierce the night,
Melodies of the vast unknown,
Each note a whisper, pure delight,
In a world that feels like home.

Underneath the fading light,
The world wraps in a blanket deep,
Stars awaken, joyous and bright,
As the arctic secrets softly seep.

In this serenade of twilight's hue,
The heart finds peace, eternally free,
With every breath, a world anew,
In the cradle of the sea and me.

Whispers of Crystal Air

Gentle breezes weave through trees,
Carrying secrets on the breeze.
Whispers soft as silken threads,
Kissing dreams where beauty treads.

Laughter dances in the light,
Painting shadows warm and bright.
Echoed songs of nature's grace,
Envelop all in soft embrace.

Floating near in sapphire skies,
Where the tranquil spirit flies.
Delicate as morning dew,
Awakening the heart anew.

Charming breezes gently shake,
Fill the world with joy awake.
Nature hums a sacred tune,
Beneath the watchful sun and moon.

In this realm where dreams are spun,
Life begins, a journey run.
Whispers of crystal air shall flow,
Guiding hearts to where they glow.

Chasing Winter's Breath

Frosted flakes in silver flight,
Twirl like dancers in the night.
Whispers echo through the pines,
Chasing winter's gentle signs.

Each breath lingers, crisp and clear,
Painting worlds we hold so dear.
Frozen petals, soft and white,
Kissing earth with pure delight.

Footsteps crunch on snow-clad trails,
With every step, adventure sails.
Winds of change, they softly call,
Awake the senses, one and all.

As twilight cloaks the snowy ground,
Magic whispers all around.
Glow of stars in deepening skies,
Breathe in winter, hear its sighs.

Chasing dreams in snowy haze,
Captured in the frosty gaze.
Winter's breath will always stay,
Woven deep in core of day.

Beneath the Silent Veil

In the quiet, shadows blend,
Whispers linger without end.
Mysteries wrapped in shades of gray,
Beneath the silent veil, they play.

Softly woven, dreams take flight,
Hidden softly, out of sight.
Flowing gently through the night,
Shrouded in the moon's soft light.

Tales of yore, secrets told,
In the hush, their truths unfold.
Silent echoes, memories swell,
Lost within the quiet spell.

Watch the stars as they align,
Threads of fate in soft design.
Beneath the silent veil we find,
The heart's desires intertwined.

In the shadows, magic brews,
Traces of the night's deep hues.
Here in silence, we will dwell,
Wandering beneath the spell.

A Tapestry of Ice

Glittering like diamonds bright,
Nature weaves in purest light.
A tapestry of ice unfolds,
Stories whispered, softly told.

Every flake, a tale of grace,
Dancing 'neath the winter's face.
Crystals spark in morning sun,
Unraveling where snowflakes run.

Fragile beauty, shimmering glow,
Painting landscapes white as snow.
In the stillness, peace is found,
In this frozen, hallowed ground.

Threads of light and shadow play,
Mark the passage of the day.
Underneath the frosty breath,
Life embraces love, not death.

Nature's canvas, vast and wide,
Hidden wonders deep inside.
In this tapestry of ice,
Lie reflections, sweet and nice.

The Serenity of Frozen Delights

Amidst the hush of snowflakes falling,
A world transformed, so calm, enthralling.
Shimmering crystals in gentle light,
Nature's wonders, a pure delight.

Footprints trace where few have tread,
In the silent woods, where whispers spread.
Cold air dances, crisp and bright,
In this embrace, all feels right.

Twinkling stars above glisten clear,
The quiet night draws dreams near.
Frozen branches, a lace of white,
Wrapped in peace, hearts take flight.

With every breath, the chill invades,
Yet warmth abounds in the heart's charades.
Cocoa sipped by fireside glow,
In serene depths, our spirits flow.

Winter's charm, a fleeting phase,
In frozen delights, we find our gaze.
To cherish moments, pure and bright,
In the serenity of winter's night.

Landscapes Painted in White

Blanketed fields, a canvas wide,
Where shadows play and secrets hide.
Every corner, untouched, serene,
Nature's art, a pristine scene.

Mountains rise with a frosted crown,
Whispers echo, the world slows down.
Pine trees stand, their crowns adorned,
In this stillness, the heart is warmed.

Sunlight glimmers on frozen lakes,
A winter's breath, as stillness aches.
Paths of white beneath the blue,
Painted landscapes, a tranquil view.

Gentle winds carry tales untold,
Of feathered friends and nights so cold.
In every drift, a story lies,
A winter's magic beneath the skies.

Nature's brush, both bold and light,
Crafting visions in endless white.
In this realm, our spirits sing,
As landscapes painted in white take wing.

Whispers of the Frozen Horizon

Softly the night cloaks the day,
Whispers float where shadows play.
Frozen echoes call our name,
In this silence, we feel the same.

Skies of azure, kissed by frost,
In nature's grip, we find the lost.
Each breath a fog, a moment stays,
As whispers weave through wintry ways.

Twilight dances with fading light,
Stars awaken, twinkling bright.
Here in the hush, we pause to dream,
Amongst the whispers, a soft gleam.

Winds of change carry tales anew,
Frozen horizons call us through.
With every step on this soft white bed,
New paths unfold as the old ones shed.

In every twinkle, every sigh,
The frozen horizon bids us fly.
A world reborn in icy grace,
In whispers quiet, we find our place.

A Dance with the Icy Dawn

Morning light breaks through the chill,
Painting the world with beauty still.
Frosted fields in hues of gold,
A fresh new day, a story told.

In the stillness, shadows play,
Nature awakens to greet the day.
Each breath a dance, a gentle sway,
As icy dawn holds night at bay.

Crisp air wraps like a soft embrace,
Footsteps crunch in this sacred space.
The sun spills warmth in radiant streams,
Awakening the land from dreams.

Trees shimmer under morning's glow,
As sunlight kisses the glistening snow.
In this moment, our spirits rise,
A dance with dawn beneath the skies.

Every second, a timeless ballet,
As winter fades to make way for May.
With hearts in sync, we joyfully fawn,
In the dance of life at the icy dawn.

Echoes in the Hushed Sky

Whispers of the night so clear,
Stars above, they shine and steer.
Moonlight dances on the ground,
In the silence, dreams are found.

Softly now, the shadows creep,
Secrets that the heavens keep.
A gentle breeze, a fleeting sigh,
Echoes linger in the sky.

In the dark, a spark of light,
Guiding wanderers of the night.
Through the stillness, time will bend,
As we walk, the paths extend.

Songs of stars, they hum and glow,
Painting tales of long ago.
In the hush, the world awakes,
Underneath the dream that breaks.

Each heartbeat in the quiet space,
Reflecting hope, a soft embrace.
With every echo, hearts will rise,
In the whispers of the skies.

Ethereal Ice in Twilight's Embrace

In twilight's arms, the world transforms,
A crystal realm where beauty warms.
Ethereal ice, so pure and bright,
Cascades of shimmer in fading light.

Beneath the glow of evening's veil,
Frosty whispers tell a tale.
Glistening paths, a silent guide,
Crafting magic in the tide.

Reflections dance on frozen streams,
Weaving together our soft dreams.
A breath of chill, a fleeting spark,
In the twilight, shadows dark.

The air so crisp, the stars ignite,
Illuminating the calm of night.
As colors blend in twilight's scheme,
We wander through a waking dream.

Every flake, a fleeting sigh,
In this realm where spirits fly.
Ethereal ice, the heart's sweet trace,
Captured in twilight's embrace.

Radiance of the Frosty Realm

In the frost, a glow emerges,
Whispers of light, the spirit urges.
Radiance shines on snowflakes bright,
Draping the world in pure delight.

Glistening trees with branches bare,
Sparkling jewels hang in the air.
Each breath forms a cloud of dreams,
In this realm, nothing's as it seems.

Echoes of laughter, joy embraced,
Time stands still in this frosty place.
With every step, a crisp delight,
Dancing shadows in the soft twilight.

The moonlit path, a shining guide,
Through the woods where wonders hide.
Stars above in silent cheer,
Illuminating what we hold dear.

Radiance blooms in winter's heart,
Capturing warmth in icy art.
Together here, our spirits rise,
In the frost beneath the skies.

Shimmering Chill at Sundown

As daylight fades, a chill descends,
The sun dips low, the sky transcends.
Shimmering hues of dusk arrive,
In this moment, dreams revive.

Soft whispers dance on evening air,
Brushing gently without a care.
A palette rich, the night unfolds,
Stories written in shades of gold.

The frost emerges, painting ground,
With every breath, a magic found.
Sundown's glow, a soft embrace,
With shimmering chill, we find our place.

In twilight's arms, the world will gleam,
Reflecting all our hidden dreams.
With every shadow, every light,
We gather close, the stars ignite.

Through the cold, our hearts will soar,
In shimmering peace, we'll explore.
As night wraps round, a tender shroud,
We find our solace in the crowd.

Glistening Thoughts on the Wind

Whispers dance in the breeze,
Carrying secrets of the trees.
Moments captured in the flight,
Glistening thoughts kissed by light.

Dreams unfold in the air,
Softly drifting without a care.
Chasing echoes, vibrant and free,
Glistening thoughts shared with me.

Patterns weave in azure skies,
Stories told without goodbyes.
A tapestry of joys and fears,
Glistening thoughts that bring us near.

Sighs awaken in silent chime,
Lingering shadows of our time.
Each breeze carries memories sweet,
Glistening thoughts, a fragrant treat.

Let the wind be our guide,
Through paths where dreams collide.
In the dance of whispers bright,
Glistening thoughts soar with delight.

Silence Wrapped in Ice

Stillness blankets the cold ground,
Echoes fade, not a sound.
Beauty rests in frosty grace,
Silence wrapped in a crystalline lace.

Shadows stretch as the sun hides,
Night descends where silence bides.
Stars shimmer in the chill of night,
Silence wrapped, a tranquil sight.

Footsteps crunch on the frozen floor,
Yearning for warmth, we explore.
Heartbeats echo, slow and nice,
In the stillness, wrapped in ice.

Time stands still, moments sigh,
In the depths where dreams lie.
Quiet whispers share their space,
Silence wrapped in nature's embrace.

Each breath a cloud in the air,
A fleeting thought, a gentle prayer.
In solitude, we find our peace,
Silence wrapped, our souls release.

Dialogues of the Winter Sky

Clouds gather like a restless sea,
Speaking hushed to you and me.
Raindrops freeze mid-air to fall,
Dialogues of the sky's soft call.

Whispers swirl in wintry breath,
Carrying tales of life and death.
Each snowflake a word unspun,
Dialogues twirl until they're done.

Stars peek through a silver veil,
Sparking stories, bold and frail.
Moonlight dances, casting glow,
Dialogues of night in silver flow.

Crisp air carries thoughts so near,
With every breeze, our hearts can hear.
In winter's grasp, we seek to fly,
Dialogues shared beneath the sky.

Snow falls gently, painting white,
Covering earth in soft delight.
Nature's whisper, oh so sly,
Dialogues woven, you and I.

A Symphony of Chilled Light

Brisk winds play a quiet tune,
Echoing softly, night to noon.
Every glimmer, a note so bright,
A symphony of chilled light.

Icicles drip like silver rhyme,
Crafted by the hands of time.
Reflections dance on winter's crest,
A symphony that never rests.

Bells of frost in a pale blue glow,
Chilling whispers in the flow.
Harmony in every flight,
A symphony of pure delight.

Hear the chorus in the trees,
Melodies born on the breeze.
Nature wakes, spirits ignite,
In a symphony of chilled light.

Together we stand, hearts aligned,
In the music where hope is found.
Let the night sing out so bright,
A symphony shared in the soft twilight.

Hues of Winter's Message

In shades of gray the world unfolds,
A canvas painted, damp and cold.
Whispers of frost on every tree,
Nature holds secrets, wild and free.

Icicles hang like crystal spears,
Reflecting hopes and hidden fears.
The silence sings, a sweet embrace,
As winter's breath reshapes the space.

Footprints trace where few have been,
Stories woven in the skin.
Flakes of snow, soft lullabies,
Gently drift beneath the skies.

Shimmering lights in darkened shades,
Guide the lost through winter glades.
Beneath the chill, warmth still survives,
In every heart, the fire thrives.

Breezes carry the scent of pine,
Welcome signs of ancient time.
In hues of white, the world is stlll,
A quiet peace, a potent thrill.

The Enchantment of Cold Breezes

Cold breezes dance through aching trees,
Whispering tales with effortless ease.
Each gust a spell, both soft and fierce,
Winter's breath, our souls it pierce.

Frosty tendrils in every nook,
Life slows down, the world it took.
As silence reigns, hearts open wide,
Seeking warmth, with dreams we bide.

A blanket spread of purest white,
Hides the world in gentle light.
Every flake a fleeting chance,
In this hush, we find romance.

Frozen echoes of laughter play,
In houses where children stay.
Magic swirls in icy air,
Winter's love, beyond compare.

Softly we turn to fireside glow,
As midnight falls and embers flow.
In chilling winds, we hold each other,
Sharing warmth, a blissful tether.

Celestial Veils of White

Under skies so vast and bright,
Lie the veils of winter's white.
Clouds cascade in a silent stream,
Wrapped in a soft, ethereal dream.

Stars peek from their crystal bed,
Illuminating paths we've tread.
Each twinkling light a gentle wink,
A dance of fate, a moment's link.

With every flake, the world anew,
Covered soft in frosted dew.
The chill of night, the warmth of day,
In winter's breath, we find our way.

A blanket hugs the sleeping earth,
Birthing moments of quiet mirth.
In shadows deep, the magic plays,
As time drifts softly, it sways.

With snowflakes falling like whispers sweet,
Nature's song beneath our feet.
In this hush, our hearts take flight,
Celestial veils, a wondrous sight.

Crystalline Wishes in Midair

Wishes float on winter's breath,
Dancing dreams that conquer death.
Crystalline glimmers, fragile and bright,
Sparkle softly in the night.

Moments trapped in frosted glass,
Time stands still, yet hours pass.
Each twirl a hope, a whispered plight,
In the embrace of soft moonlight.

Chasing shadows, fingers trace,
Magic held in every space.
In the stillness, we find our way,
Crystalline wishes gently sway.

Silent prayers to skies of gray,
For love and joy, come what may.
Beneath the snow, our hopes align,
All intertwined, forever shine.

As winter melts into the spring,
We hold these wishes, take to wing.
In every flake, a dream takes flight,
Crystalline wishes, pure delight.

Dreams Dressed in Silver

In the night, stars softly gleam,
Whispers float like a silver stream.
Thoughts take flight, like birds in grace,
Dancing gently in a luminous space.

Moonlit paths call out my name,
Through the mist, I feel no shame.
Each wish cast in the night's embrace,
Shimmers bright in time's gentle chase.

In this realm where shadows play,
Hope ignites, lighting the way.
Dreams wrapped tight in a silver thread,
Guide my heart where my soul is led.

Stars align in perfect rhyme,
Carving moments out of time.
With every breath, a promise grows,
In the stillness, my spirit flows.

Awake or lost in sweetest dreams,
Everything is not what it seems.
Clad in silver, draped in light,
I'll wander on through the endless night.

Soft Hues of a Frozen Canvas

On a canvas kissed by frost,
Gentle hues, beauty embossed.
Each shade whispers of winter's grace,
Painting stories in a quiet place.

The world is hushed beneath the snow,
Dancing flakes in a silent flow.
Trees adorned with glistening white,
Stand as sentinels in the night.

A palette rich with chill and glow,
Echoes of nature's gentle show.
Frozen dreams held in a glance,
In the stillness, where shadows dance.

The dawn breaks soft, a tender light,
Bathing the earth in warmth so bright.
Colors blend in a subtle song,
In this realm where we all belong.

As the day fades, the hues will shift,
Magic wrapped in nature's gift.
Soft whispers of a frozen land,
Hold the dreams we understand.

Twilight's Icy Caress

Underneath a twilight sky,
Stars awaken, softly shy.
Icy breezes brush my face,
Whispers linger in their grace.

Glimmers of light begin to blend,
Where day meets night, shadows send.
A chill embraces every sigh,
Painting skies where dreams can fly.

Frozen whispers tease the ear,
In this twilight, all is clear.
Moments pause, still time stands still,
As the heart embraces thrill.

The world transformed in lavender hues,
Nurturing hopes, igniting muse.
Beneath the blanket of soft chill,
The spirit dances, free, until.

Night unfolds its silken thread,
In the calm, all fear is shed.
With twilight's icy breath so near,
I find solace, I hold dear.

Beneath a Glistening Whisper

Underneath the twilight's glow,
Glistening whispers come and go.
Secrets shared with the moonlit night,
In the stillness, hearts take flight.

Starlit paths weave stories old,
Mysteries in silence told.
With every breath, a wish is spun,
In this realm where dreams are run.

Softly now, the echoes play,
Guiding souls along the way.
Beneath the curtain of night's embrace,
Hope and love find their place.

Through glistening leaves and shadows deep,
A promise lingers, secrets keep.
Where every glance can spark a flame,
In this quiet, nothing's the same.

In whispered tones, the world unfolds,
With tales of wonder, yet untold.
Beneath a sky of shimmering light,
I find my way through the soft night.

Nurtured by the Winter's Kiss

Snowflakes dance on whispered winds,
Each flake tells a tale of peace.
Beneath the frost, life gently sleeps,
Waiting for the sun's warm release.

Branches bare, yet dreams unfold,
Silent nights in blankets white.
Stars above, like secrets told,
Glisten in the velvet night.

In the hush, a heartbeat waits,
A promise wrapped in icy care.
Hope arises; life awaits,
To break the winter's timeless snare.

Muffled sounds of nature's grace,
Softly echo through the trees.
Winter's charm, a warm embrace,
Cradles life in gentle freeze.

As the thaw begins to glow,
Colors peek from under snow.
Nature breathes a sigh of bliss,
Nurtured gently by the kiss.

Musing on a Silvered Horizon

Where the sky meets the quiet earth,
Whispers of the dawn are spun.
Dreams take flight in gentle mirth,
Underneath the waking sun.

Cotton clouds drift softly by,
Their shadows dance on fields of gold.
A canvas vast, where hopes can fly,
Musing on stories yet untold.

In the light of morning's glow,
Find solace in this fleeting hue.
Silvered edge where moments flow,
Time suspended, fresh and new.

Birds in chorus fill the air,
Songs of joy on whispered breeze.
Nature's heart, so free and fair,
Crafts a world that aims to please.

So gaze upon that silver line,
Where earth and sky in union meet.
In this space, a spark divine,
Awakens life beneath our feet.

Soft Echoes Beneath a Frigid Dome

Underneath the icy arc,
Whispers linger, soft and clear.
Stars above, a glimmering spark,
Guiding dreams from far and near.

Silent snow on branches bows,
Nature wrapped in winter's shroud.
Breath of cold, the stillness vows,
To hold the world beneath its crowd.

Echoes fade in crystal air,
Chilled reflections softly play.
Within the hush, a tender care,
Cradles night and welcomes day.

Frosted whispers weave through trees,
A lullaby for hearts that yearn.
In this dome, the spirit frees,
To dance and spin, rejoice, and learn.

With every flicker, shadows flit,
Each moment holds a silken thread.
Beneath the dome where echoes sit,
Stories bloom, and dreams are fed.

Lights Flickering on Icy Veils

Flickering lights on winter's breath,
Dancing flames in the frosty night.
Each one whispers tales of death,
And life anew in purest light.

Twinkling gems on icy streams,
Painting worlds with their soft glow.
Cascading down like fleeting dreams,
They shimmer gently, ebb and flow.

Frosted whispers in the air,
Carry secrets of the past.
Each bright spark, a tender prayer,
Wishing for the love to last.

Snowflakes swirl in a mystic dance,
Underneath the night's embrace.
In their grace, a fleeting chance,
To find the warmth in coldest space.

So let the lights guide your path,
Through the veil of winter's chill.
In their flickers, find your heart,
And let their glow your spirit fill.

Celestial Whispers of the North

In the hush of night so clear,
Stars above softly appear.
A gentle breeze begin to sing,
Of winter's love and all it brings.

Moonlight dances on the snow,
Casting shadows, soft and slow.
Whispers of the north take flight,
Guiding souls through the night.

Frosty breath paints trees in white,
While echoes glow in pale starlight.
Nature's quilt, a sacred trust,
Wrapped in dreams, a world of dust.

Every flake tells a tale of ice,
Frigid moments, soft and nice.
Heaven's canvas, vast and wide,
In its beauty, we abide.

Underneath this darkened veil,
Secrets linger, dreams set sail.
Celestial whispers fill the air,
A cosmic dance beyond compare.

The Elegance of Frigid Moments

Chill bites softly at my skin,
Yet in this frost, I feel within.
The world adorned in crystal lace,
Nature's breath, a fleeting grace.

Stillness reigns where shadows play,
In winter's grasp, I long to stay.
Elegance drapes on trees so tall,
As twilight whispers a frosty call.

Every moment laced with time,
Mountains echo a silent rhyme.
Magic swirls in the cold night air,
Holding memories, tender and rare.

Dew drops glisten like tiny stars,
Nature's jewelry, no matter how far.
In such beauty, my heart finds home,
In frozen dreams, forever to roam.

Each frigid breath, a sigh of peace,
Where worries fade, our hopes increase.
With open arms, I greet the night,
In winter's elegance, pure delight.

Caresses of the Shivering Sky

Above, the sky wears a shroud,
A canvas gray, shifting, proud.
Clouds embrace the chill with grace,
Whispers of winter, a tight embrace.

Snowflakes dance and twirl away,
In the quiet of the day.
Each caress, a touch of gold,
In arms of frost, stories unfold.

A tapestry of white and gray,
Nature's breath, a soft ballet.
The horizon glows with pastel hues,
Awakening dreams, fresh to muse.

Frosted leaves with edges bright,
Softly gleaming, pure delight.
Each moment holds a shivering sigh,
In this magic, we dare to fly.

As night descends, the stars ignite,
A symphony of silence, pure night.
Caresses linger, sweet and light,
In the shivering sky, all feels right.

A Mosaic of Twilight Frost

Twilight whispers secrets low,
As day and night begin to flow.
The frost lays down a silver quilt,
Painting dreams, gentle and built.

Each breath of air, crisp and clear,
Echoes of winter linger near.
A mosaic forms on every pane,
Expressions of nature, bold yet plain.

Magic weaves through branches bare,
Tangled whispers dance in the air.
Every flake a part of art,
In this twilight, it warms the heart.

Rivers glisten, still and slow,
Mirroring skies, a tender glow.
In the hush, secrets find their way,
Softly spoken, night turns to day.

Frost wraps gently, softly tight,
Creating worlds in fading light.
In a mosaic of twilight, we see,
The beauty of nature, wild and free.

Ethereal Blue of Winter's Realm

In whispers soft, the blue unfolds,
A canvas vast where silence holds.
The chill runs deep through branches bare,
As frost-kissed dreams weave through the air.

The twilight glows, a fleeting sight,
As shadows dance with fading light.
The stars peek through the icy veil,
In winter's grasp, the night will sail.

A tranquil hush, the world serene,
In this cold realm, a mystic scene.
Where time stands still, and hearts can roam,
In ethereal blue, we find our home.

Glistening Clouds of Icy Wonder

Above the earth, the clouds drift by,
With glistening shapes that catch the eye.
They sparkle bright in silver light,
A wondrous sight, a pure delight.

Beneath them lies a world aglow,
Where whispers of the winter blow.
The crisp, clean air, a subtle tease,
As nature sleeps with gentle ease.

These icy dreams the heavens send,
A fleeting touch, a soft descend.
In wonder, we embrace the chill,
As clouds of ice weave time, be still.

Beneath the Shimmering Expanse

Beneath the sky, so vast and bright,
We wander through the winter's night.
The stars above, a dance of fate,
In shimmering hues, we meditate.

The frost beneath our feet does crunch,
Each step a melody, a subtle punch.
The midnight air, a biting kiss,
In this still world, we find our bliss.

Whispers of secrets softly told,
Through winter's song, our hearts unfold.
In nature's grasp, we linger long,
Beneath the expanse, a timeless song.

A Tapestry of Ice and Dream

A tapestry where dreams entwine,
In icy threads, our hopes align.
Each crystalline flake, a tale to tell,
In winter's embrace, we know it well.

The world transformed, so pure and white,
Beneath the stars, a tranquil sight.
With every breath, the magic swells,
In frozen art, our spirit dwells.

A dance of frost upon the ground,
In silence deep, true peace is found.
We weave our dreams with every sigh,
In this tapestry, we learn to fly.

Celestial Shards in the Evening

In the twilight hue, the stars ignite,
Whispers of dusk, a soft delight.
Shards of light dance in the air,
Painting dreams without a care.

Silhouettes of trees stand tall,
Guardians of night, they enthrall.
Moonlight weaves through branches bare,
A tender touch, a gentler glare.

Colors fade, the shadows grow,
Cascading hues, a nightly show.
In this realm where silence sings,
The evening breathes, the dark one clings.

Lost in wonder, hearts take flight,
Guided gently by the night.
Celestial shards, a jeweled sky,
A serenade, as time slips by.

Moments linger, soft and sweet,
Echoes of stars, quiet retreat.
In this magic, souls entwine,
Underneath the vast design.

Starcrest of the Frosty Night

Above the world, the cosmos glows,
A frosty breath, the starlight flows.
Each twinkle tells a tale untold,
Of whispered dreams and hearts of gold.

The winter air, a crystal breeze,
Beneath the trees, the soft snow flees.
Beneath the heavens, silent paths,
Awake with joy, as laughter laughs.

Chill of night, the stars awake,
Bright against the cold sky's stake.
A silent watch, they gleam and shine,
In every moment, stories entwine.

Footprints trace on frozen ground,
Echoes of love, silently found.
In this starcrest, peace takes flight,
Holding tight to the frosty night.

Whispers weave through the glittered light,
Telling tales of eternal flight.
In the embrace of dark and bright,
We find our way in the velvet night.

Glacial Embrace of Dusk

As day bids farewell, the sky blushes,
Mountains shrouded in twilight's hushes.
Glacial visions, serene and grand,
Caress the earth with a tender hand.

Whispers of ice in the quiet air,
Nature's peace, beauty laid bare.
In the fading light, shadows extend,
Teasing the thoughts that time cannot bend.

Stars emerge in a captivating dance,
Inviting dreamers to take a chance.
With each breath, a frozen sigh,
In the glacial embrace, we gently lie.

Warmth of hearts in the chilly pall,
Echoes of night, beckoning all.
Wrapped in silence, we find a space,
Where memories linger, a soft embrace.

In dusk's embrace, the world stands still,
Filling the night with a quiet thrill.
Glacial shadows in the fading hue,
Remind us softly of love so true.

Serenade of the Silver Morn

As dawn unfolds with gentle grace,
A silver sheen on nature's face.
Birdsong echoes, sweet and clear,
Whispers of day that draw us near.

The mist rises, a soft embrace,
A fleeting moment, time's sweet trace.
In the light of day, all is reborn,
With laughter bright, the world is worn.

Golden rays break through the night,
Chasing shadows, bringing light.
In the dance of leaves, a whispered tune,
Serenading hearts with the sun and moon.

Each petal glimmers with morning dew,
A canvas alive, fresh and new.
In the harmony of life, we find,
A serenade that heals the mind.

As silver morn greets the sky,
With dreams awake, we learn to fly.
In the embrace of dawn's sweet song,
We find our place, where we belong.

Glimmers of the Twilight

The sun dips low, a radiant hue,
Whispers of night begin to ensue.
Stars awaken in the jeweled sky,
Softly painting dreams as they fly.

Shadows stretch on the cool, damp ground,
Nature sighs, in peace it is found.
Glimmers dance on the flowing stream,
A tranquil canvas, a painter's dream.

The breeze carries secrets of old,
Stories in twilight, quietly told.
Moonlight weaves through the branches above,
Wrapping the world in a tender love.

With each heartbeat, the silence swells,
Echoes of magic the twilight spells.
Hearts intertwined in this fleeting hour,
Beneath the heavens, we feel the power.

In this moment, all worries cease,
Nature cradles us, offering peace.
Glimmers of twilight softly unfold,
As dreams ignite with the light of gold.

The Chill of Distant Horizons

The horizon whispers its frosty breath,
A chill descends, a dance with death.
Mountains loom, cloaked in icy white,
Silent witnesses of fading light.

Clouds gather, dark as a secret tide,
Veiling the warmth that once did bide.
Cold winds howl through the barren trees,
Carrying tales of forgotten seas.

Footsteps crunch on the frozen ground,
Each one echoes, a haunting sound.
A journey starts, though the path is steep,
Into the night where shadows creep.

The chill envelops like a ghostly shroud,
Nature sleeps beneath her winter cloud.
Stars flicker, faint as they watch us roam,
Guiding us back to the warmth of home.

In distance waits a flicker of dawn,
Hope's whisper calls as night is withdrawn.
With every step into the unknown,
The chill retreats, and courage has grown.

Luminous Echoes at Dusk

The sun bows low, a golden goodbye,
Colors meld in a soft, sweet sigh.
Crimson and violet paint the skies,
As the day gently fades and quiet lies.

Echoes of laughter drift on the breeze,
Beneath the trees, amidst the leaves.
Memories shimmer like stars in the night,
Luminous whispers, a heart's delight.

Candles flicker on window sills,
Softening shadows, igniting thrills.
In the hush of dusk, dreams intertwine,
Cradled in warmth that's tender and fine.

The horizon glows with a tender hue,
Seasons change, but our hearts stay true.
Moments linger beneath the twilight,
Whispers of love, a gentle light.

In this embrace of day and night,
We find solace, a shared respite.
Luminous echoes in fading light,
Guide us gently into the night.

Celestial Frost and Dreams

In the stillness of a frozen dawn,
Celestial frost begins to yawn.
Crystals glisten on the windowpanes,
A world transformed, where magic reigns.

Dreams take flight on the winter air,
Whispers of hope, a delicate prayer.
Stars twinkle bright in the velvet night,
Guided by wishes, shimmering light.

The moon stands guard over slumbering earth,
Cradling secrets of nature's birth.
With every breath, the cosmos sings,
A symphony soft as the dawn's first wings.

In the frost, we've woven our tales,
Of love and courage that never pales.
Each twinkling star a promise made,
In celestial dreams, our fears will fade.

Embrace the night, let your spirit soar,
In this frosted realm, you're evermore.
Celestial frost will guide your way,
As dreams awaken with the light of day.

Snow-Kissed Horizons

The dawn breaks soft and white,
A canvas fresh and bright.
Mountains wear a veil of snow,
Whispers of the winds blow.

Footprints trace a secret path,
Nature's silent, gentle math.
Each crystal sparkles in the light,
Snow-kissed horizons, pure delight.

The frost adorns the sleeping ground,
In frozen stillness, peace is found.
A world wrapped in winter's embrace,
Time and space, a gentle chase.

As shadows lengthen on the land,
We marvel at the silent hand.
Snowflakes dance, a fleeting sight,
In this cold, our hearts take flight.

Evening whispers soft and low,
Painting skies in twilight glow.
With every sigh, a secret shared,
Snow-kissed horizons, souls laid bare.

Luminous Chill of Twilight

Twilight weaves its silver thread,
A gentle chill where dreams are fed.
Stars awaken in the dark,
A luminous glow, a spark.

The sky blushes, deep indigo,
As whispers of the night do flow.
Shadows dance beneath the trees,
Carried softly on the breeze.

The moon peeks through a veil of mist,
In quiet moments, dreams persist.
A tapestry of light and dark,
Through every heartbeat, every lark.

The chill embraces restless minds,
In nature's fold, solace finds.
Together with the starry skies,
We find the truth in gentle sighs.

Luminous chill, a magic veil,
In twilight's breath, we find the trail.
A path where whispers softly glide,
In this embrace, we safely bide.

Wings of Ice on Whispering Winds

Wings of ice caress the air,
Gliding softly without a care.
Whispers ride on frosty streams,
Carrying the weight of dreams.

Crystal feathers, pure and bright,
Twirl and twine in morning light.
Nature's breath, a soft refrain,
Echoes in the winter's bane.

The world below, so still and white,
Cradles whispers of delight.
Every flake a story spun,
A mosaic bright under the sun.

High above, the moments soar,
Graceful paths forevermore.
A union of the earth and sky,
In this realm, we learn to fly.

Wings of ice, with beauty blessed,
In this dance, our hearts find rest.
As winds carry us far and wide,
In winter's arms, we safely bide.

Radiant Frost above Silent Trees

Radiant frost cloaks every branch,
A jeweled gown, the trees' own dance.
Silent whispers fill the air,
Nature's secret, pure and rare.

With every breath, the world holds tight,
To dreams that shimmer in the light.
A tapestry of white and grey,
Guiding hearts to find their way.

Underneath the frosted crown,
Silent whispers hint and drown.
Each heartbeat sings beneath the sky,
Woven tales that softly fly.

Amidst the calm and quiet grace,
Timeless beauty finds its place.
In winter's spell, we stand so still,
Chasing echoes, hearts to fill.

Radiant frost, a spark divine,
In nature's arms, our souls entwine.
Silent trees watch over all,
In their presence, we never fall.

Celestial Whispers in Winter Light

In the hush of winter nights,
Stars twinkle with secrets bright,
Moonlight dances on the snow,
Whispers travel, soft and slow.

Frosty breaths adorn the air,
Nature pauses, unaware,
Trees stand tall, a silent choir,
Echoing dreams, a world afire.

Each flake falls with grace, serene,
A memory wrapped in white sheen,
Underneath this twilight dome,
Hearts find peace, and wander home.

In shadows cast by silver beams,
Life unfolds in quiet dreams,
Gentle breeze through branches sways,
Guiding souls in winter's haze.

The nightingale's last song is heard,
A lullaby, soft and blurred,
Celestial whispers, pure delight,
Carried forth in winter light.

Ethereal Hues of the Chill

Beneath a sky of muted gray,
The world transforms, night and day,
Ethereal hues in icy streams,
Nature wraps us in her dreams.

Silent forests dressed in frost,
Whispers of warmth, never lost,
Color fades to softest white,
Painting moments, pure delight.

Icicles hang like crystal chains,
Glimmers spark in window panes,
Chilly winds the branches tease,
Nature's breath, a frozen breeze.

Each step cracks through powdered snow,
Secrets of the earth below,
Echoes blend in softest sighs,
Winter's magic never lies.

In every flake, a story unfurls,
Of distant lands and frozen swirls,
Ethereal hues, so rich and bright,
Basking in the glow of light.

Illuminated Shadows of Winter

When sun meets snow in soft embrace,
Illuminated shadows trace,
Cool blue tones, a dance so fine,
Nature's canvas, pure divine.

Glistening fields underfoot,
Footprints left, in silence, root,
Shadows stretch through fading light,
Keeping warmth against the night.

Branches bare against the sky,
Whispers of where dreams may lie,
Songs of winter, crisp and clear,
In the stillness, hearts draw near.

Crimson sunsets fade away,
Stars ignite in grand display,
Illuminated paths we tread,
With every thought, a word unsaid.

In winter's grasp, we find our way,
Through illuminated shadows, play,
Each moment sacred, every breath,
In the beauty found in death.

A Glint Above the Snowy Woods

Above the trees, a soft glint shines,
Moonlight spills in silver lines,
Through branches bare, the stars peep down,
Gifting the world a celestial crown.

Snow wraps hills in a shimmering coat,
Nature hums, a gentle note,
Each sparkle laid like diamonds rare,
In the midnight, a tranquil air.

Frosted whispers fill the night,
Echoes of joy, pure delight,
A symphony of peace resounds,
In the quiet, love abounds.

Wanderers pause to gaze and dream,
Caught in winter's fleeting gleam,
Moments captured, hearts set free,
In the magic of what's to be.

In the stillness, truth is found,
A glint that holds the world unbound,
Above the woods, where silence reigns,
Winter's heart forever gains.

Dancing with Ghosts of Ice

In the moonlit night, shadows sway,
Whispers of frost in a delicate ballet.
Each step echoes, soft and clear,
Swaying gently, the spirits near.

Frosted breath hangs in the air,
Icicles glisten, a beauty rare.
Chilled fingers trace on frozen glass,
In this moment, together we pass.

Silhouettes twirl through the silent trees,
Their laughter carried by the winter breeze.
Dancing softly with memories past,
In the stillness, their shadows cast.

Crystalline dreams swirl in the night,
Awakening wonder in pale moonlight.
A ghostly waltz that knows no end,
In the embrace of time, we blend.

When dawn breaks, the spirits fade,
But the chill in the air, they have made.
Lingering echoes in the morning mist,
Ghosts of ice in the sunshine kissed.

Fragmented Reflections on White

A canvas blank, untouched by time,
Snowflakes whisper, soft as a rhyme.
Each flake a memory, falling light,
Painting the world in hues of white.

Mirrored surfaces, so stark and bright,
Reflecting dreams in fractured light.
In this moment, a stillness found,
A breath of silence, profound.

Footprints lead through the endless snow,
Chasing thoughts where cold winds blow.
Fleeting moments, swift as a blink,
In the solitude, we pause and think.

Underneath the pale sky's dome,
We find a place that feels like home.
Whispers of winter, stories unfold,
In shards of beauty, tales retold.

Fragmented reflections, sharp and clear,
Echoes of laughter, fading near.
In the silence, we engage the light,
Finding warmth in the depths of white.

The Kiss of a Chilled Horizon

At dawn's first light, the world awakes,
A chilled horizon, where silence breaks.
Colors bleed into the morning air,
A tranquil moment, beyond compare.

Beneath the frost, the earth lies still,
Life's warm heartbeat, a constant thrill.
As sunlight kisses the frosted land,
Nature breathes softly, hand in hand.

Clouds dance lightly across the sky,
Fleeting shadows drift and sigh.
The earth wrapped in a crystalline shawl,
A hush envelops, as whispers call.

A chilly breeze carries tales untold,
Of seasons past and winters bold.
Each breath a promise of days to come,
In the stillness, a gentle hum.

The horizon glimmers, kissed by light,
A symphony of beauty, day from night.
In dawn's embrace, warmth starts to rise,
The world awakens under painted skies.

Visuals of a Frosty Daydream

In the hush of dawn, a vision glows,
Frosty dreams wrapped in gentle throws.
Veils of mist dance on frozen streams,
Where everything sparkles, a world of dreams.

Soft whispers glide through the fields of white,
Nature's canvas, a breathtaking sight.
Textures shimmer, soft and surreal,
In this daydream, we can feel.

The sun peeks through, a radiant ray,
Painting shadows that sway and play.
A tapestry woven with silver thread,
In the stillness, all worries shed.

Snowflakes twirl like thoughts in the air,
Fleeting memories everywhere.
Holding close what the heart does seek,
In a frosty daydream, soft and meek.

Visuals bloom in a winter's grasp,
Moments like jewels, we yearn to clasp.
A gentle reminder, nature's song,
In the chill of magic, we all belong.

Glistening Dreams beneath Starlit Haze

In the quiet night we wait,
Whispers in the cool, soft breeze.
Stars like diamonds, they illuminate,
Glistening dreams bring hearts at ease.

Underneath a cosmic quilt,
Hopeful wishes take their flight.
Every twinkle, every wilt,
Promising serenity tonight.

The moon watches, silver and wise,
Casting shadows on our fate.
In this symphony of skies,
We find love, we celebrate.

In the stillness, time stands still,
As wishes drift from star to star.
Embracing magic, bending will,
Together, we shall wander far.

With stardust sprinkled in our eyes,
We walk paths of dreams so bright.
In this realm where hope aligns,
Glistening dreams guide us tonight.

Reflective Echoes in the Chill

In the silent woods we tread,
Breath visible like clouds of thought.
Amidst the trees, a tale is spread,
Reflective echoes gently caught.

Whispers rustle through the leaves,
Tales of those who came before.
Every step, the heart believes,
Echoes beckon, urging more.

Frosted patterns on the ground,
Nature's art, a fleeting gift.
Within the chill, we are bound,
Feeling time's unyielding drift.

Shadows dance as twilight falls,
Footsteps linger in the night.
Each echo in silence calls,
Guiding souls to distant light.

In this moment, we embrace,
Reflections glisten in our minds.
The chill becomes a warm embrace,
In echoes, solace we find.

The Icy Touch of Celestial Spheres

Above us glows the endless night,
Celestial spheres, bright and bold.
Their icy touch brings pure delight,
A tapestry of dreams retold.

With galaxies that twist and turn,
Each star a whisper from afar.
In cosmic light, our spirits burn,
Connected like the night's bright star.

Nebulas of colors rich and rare,
Painting the darkness with their hues.
The icy touch we gladly bear,
In their glow, we find our muse.

Planets spin in perfect dance,
Orbiting with a timeless grace.
They lure us with their mystic trance,
Embracing dreams in their vast space.

In the stillness of the vast expanse,
We reach our hands to touch the sky.
The icy touch, a cosmic chance,
In celestial realms, we fly.

Winter's Breath on a Silhouetted Sky

As the sun dips low, shadows grow,
A silhouetted sky unfolds.
Winter's breath begins to blow,
Whispers of warmth in the cold.

Trees stand tall against the dusk,
Branches bare, a stark ballet.
In the stillness, there's a husk,
A promise of the light of day.

With each breath a cloud appears,
Carrying the chill of night.
Yet in this moment, calm and clear,
Hope lingers in soft twilight.

Snowflakes dance like fragile dreams,
Caught in winter's gentle hand.
Beneath the sky, a realm it seems,
Where stillness whispers across the land.

In the quiet, hearts unite,
Holding warmth against the freeze.
Winter's breath ignites the night,
A silhouetted world at peace.

The Tranquil Gaze of a Frozen Dawn

The snowflakes dance in morning light,
A world aglow, bathed soft and white.
Whispers of dawn through branches weave,
In frozen peace, our hearts believe.

A canvas fresh, untouched by time,
As daylight breaks, a quiet rhyme.
Each crystal shimmer, a silent song,
In nature's own, where we belong.

The breath of winter, crisp and clear,
In stillness found, a moment dear.
With every step, the world transforms,
In tranquil gaze, the heart conforms.

A fleeting moment, yet profound,
In frozen hush, we seek the sound.
Nature's heart, it beats so slow,
As day unfolds in softest glow.

Beneath the sky, so vast and wide,
We find our dreams where shadows hide.
In every breath, a silent bond,
With frozen dawn, our souls respond.

Celestial Chill in Starlit Silence

Night cascades with a silver hue,
Stars above, a celestial view.
Bathed in chill, the air feels light,
Whispers of dreams take gentle flight.

Each twinkle tells a tale once lost,
The universe, we bear its cost.
In the stillness, secrets shared,
A bond unspoken, deeply cared.

Beneath the vast and endless sky,
The heart reflects a soft, sweet sigh.
Moments captured in starlit grace,
A cosmic dance; a timeless space.

The chill of night invites the calm,
In silence deep, we find our balm.
Each star a dream, each night our guide,
In cosmic waves, our hearts abide.

As time drifts by, we lost in thought,
Each breath a treasure, deeply sought.
In starlit silence, we weave our fate,
Celestial chill, we contemplate.

The Crystal Canopy of Evening

The twilight paints the world in gray,
Where shadows dance at close of day.
Beneath the trees, the whispers hum,
In crystal light, the night will come.

Each leaf aglow, a fragile spark,
In evening's hold, dispelling dark.
The moon ascends on velvet wings,
A silver crown, the nightingale sings.

The stars emerge, a jeweled sea,
In evening's calm, we seek to be.
With every breath, a world unfolds,
In crystal canopy, the heart beholds.

As shadows stretch and silence grows,
The gentle night in stillness flows.
We find our place, beneath the skies,
In evening's warmth, where memory lies.

And as the darkness softly weaves,
A tapestry of autumn leaves.
In peaceful breaths, the soul ignites,
In crystal canopy of nights.

Glimmering Veils of Frozen Dreams

In winter's grasp, the world adorned,
With glimmering veils, the earth reborn.
Each flake a whisper, shimmers bright,
In frozen dreams, we find the light.

As daylight fades, the stars awake,
A tapestry that night will make.
Beneath the glow of pale moon's beam,
We walk in wonder, lost in dream.

Veils of ice, a crystal dance,
In nature's trance, we take our chance.
With every step, the world's ensemble,
In snowy silence, thoughts do ramble.

The night descends, a quiet pause,
In frozen realms, we seek the cause.
In gentle breaths, our spirits gleam,
Held tight within, our frozen dream.

As morning breaks, the veil gives way,
To golden hues of a brand new day.
With every dawn, a promise seams,
In glimmering veils of frozen dreams.

Illusions of the Winter Sky

The clouds drift slow and sly,
Painting dreams on winter's breath.
A tapestry of cold, they lie,
Whispers of a fading death.

Beneath the pale, soft moon's glow,
Stars flicker like forgotten sighs.
In the hush, the cool winds blow,
Telling tales of hallowed lies.

Ghostly shadows dance and weave,
In the crisp embrace of night.
They beckon us to believe,
In the magic of the light.

As frost drapes each sleeping tree,
Silence wraps the earth so tight.
We lose ourselves, set free,
In the mystique of cold delight.

The winter sky holds all our dreams,
In illusions pure and clear.
Nothing is as it seems,
Yet still, we linger here.

Stars Within an Icy Embrace

Glimmers twinkle through the night,
In shadows cast by silver beams.
Frozen whispers take flight,
Embracing all our secret dreams.

Underneath a blanket of ice,
Stars smile with a knowing gleam.
Each one holds a secret's price,
A mystery wrapped in a dream.

The chill wraps tight around the heart,
In every glance, a silent plea.
As the universe plays its part,
We find solace in the sea.

A cosmic dance beneath the stars,
With icy fingers tracing fate.
In frozen worlds too close to spar,
Love lingers in the quiet state.

In this embrace, we lose our fears,
Frosty breath upon the night.
For every moment holds the years,
Stars shine on with gentle light.

Whispered Secrets Beneath a Frozen Glow

Beneath the chill of endless night,
Secrets lie in shadows deep.
Whispers dance in silver light,
While the world around us sleeps.

Frosted branches home to dreams,
Captured in each breath we take.
Magic flows in icy streams,
In the silence, soft and wake.

Every flake a story told,
Of the warmth that lies within.
In winter's heart, we find the gold,
Where new journeys soon begin.

Muffled echoes of the past,
For the footprints soon erased.
Underneath the layer cast,
New adventures are embraced.

Twilight glimmers, time stands still,
Crystals glisten, fate bestowed.
In the night, we feel the thrill,
Of whispered secrets softly flowed.

Shards of Light on a Chilly Canvas

Morning breaks with shards of light,
    Painting frost into a dream.
Each gleam a spark of pure delight,
Upon the earth, a shimmering theme.

    Colors dance on icy streams,
    Reflecting visions of the dawn.
    Nature wakes, igniting beams,
    The chilly canvas softly drawn.

Beneath the haze of frosted air,
    Life emerges, fresh and bright.
With every breath, a silent prayer,
For warmth to conquer winter's bite.

Intricate designs form and fade,
    Artistry in nature's hands.
Echoes of the cold parade,
Across the realm of frozen lands.

In this beauty, still we find,
    Shards of hope in every sight.
With every heartbeat, intertwined,
    We embrace the winter's light.

A Starlit Tinge of Winter

The moon whispers soft, glowing bright,
Draped in a blanket of shimmering white.
Stars glimmer like diamonds on frost,
Silent dreams of warmth, never lost.

Breath in the air, crisp and cold,
Stories of winter simply told.
Each flake a memory, unique and small,
Nature's embrace, a silvery shawl.

Footprints trace paths on the ground,
In this stillness, peace is found.
Whispers of night sing through the trees,
As shadows dance with the evening breeze.

The world lies still, wrapped in grace,
Time slows down in this tranquil place.
A starlit tinge on every face,
In winter's heart, we find our space.

Hope glimmers like stars in the night,
Guiding our hearts with gentle light.
Through the cold, we wander and roam,
In winter's arms, we find our home.

In the Embrace of Chilling Clarity

The morning sun breaks, soft and clear,
In the chill, all worries disappear.
Frost-kissed branches, twinkling bright,
Whispers of dawn, a joyful sight.

Air so fresh, it fills the soul,
Every breath, a moment to hold.
In this stillness, life feels pure,
Each heartbeat echoes, strong and sure.

Snowflakes drift with delicate grace,
Painting the world, a soft embrace.
In this beauty, we find our way,
Comforted by the light of day.

Nature sings with a crystal tone,
Reminds us we're never alone.
Beneath the sky, we take our stand,
In winter's hug, hand in hand.

Moments wrap like a tender quilt,
In chilling clarity, love is spilt.
Together we brave the cold embrace,
Finding warmth in this sacred space.

Memories of the Icy Cosmos

Stars above like grains of sand,
Whispers of time from distant lands.
Each glimmer holds a story to share,
In the icy cosmos, dreams lay bare.

Galaxies swirl in elegance high,
Drawing our thoughts to the midnight sky.
In frozen stillness, we find our place,
Lost in the wonder, we drift through space.

Comets blaze with transient fire,
Reminding us of hopes and desire.
We reach for the images, bright and bold,
In memories of the cosmos, stories are told.

Time unravels beneath cosmic streams,
We chase our wishes, born from dreams.
Amidst the cold, our spirits soar,
In the icy cosmos, we long for more.

Moments frozen, tender and rare,
Each flicker of light, a timeless prayer.
In the vastness, we feel so alive,
In the heart of winter, our dreams thrive.

Veils of White Overhead

A soft hush blankets the earth below,
Veils of white in a gentle flow.
Nature's canvas, pristine and bright,
Whispers of winter dance through the night.

Trees wear coats of shimmering rime,
In their beauty, we pause for time.
Footsteps echo on fresh-fallen snow,
In every glance, a new wonder to know.

Clouds caress the sky, heavy and low,
Shrouding the world in a tranquil glow.
With every breath, a lingering sigh,
Veils of white whisper goodbye.

Children laugh, their joy in the air,
Building dreams without a care.
Each snowball tossed, a memory created,
In winter's arms, feeling elated.

Evenings bring stars, bright and keen,
Painting the shadows with silvery sheen.
Veils of white, a soft lullaby,
In the stillness, our spirits fly.

Elysian Grays

Whispers of twilight, softened and slow,
Painting the silence with shadows that flow.
Faded embers dance in the chill of the air,
Dreams intertwine where the lost spirits care.

Branches like fingers, outstretched with grace,
Holding the remnants of time's warm embrace.
Elysian hues beneath a tattered sky,
Yearning for echoes that silently die.

Crimson horizons bleed into night,
Sparks of remembrance revive fragile light.
In this moment frozen, we search and we feel,
A world wrapped in wonder, a heart that can heal.

Cascading whispers weave tales of the lost,
Delicate threads worth every cost.
Embrace the stillness, let your worries part,
For in these grays, we paint every heart.

Under the sheen of a faded moon's light,
We wander through shadows, chasing the night.
And there in the distance, we glimpse what we seek,
A harmony found when our voices grow weak.

Shards of a Frigid Dawn

Beyond the horizon, the ink starts to break,
Fractured reflections, a chilling heartache.
Frost-kissed whispers in the quiet before,
Awakening shadows, lost stories to explore.

Hope flickers gently, a soft, fleeting ray,
Crystals of sunlight begin to betray.
Each shard of the dawn, a promise undone,
Echoes of warmth in the chill of the sun.

Glistening fragments, like dreams left behind,
Shimmer and quiver, in silence they bind.
The air, a canvas where memories play,
Sketching the paths of a forgotten day.

Birds take to flight, their shadows unite,
Across the cold canvas, their delicate sight.
In the shattering dawn, we piece together,
The warmth we desire, the love we remember.

Beneath the bleak canvas, the colors will bloom,
Lifting our spirits, dispelling the gloom.
With each shard of truth, a new vision appears,
Transforming our fears into hopeful cheers.

Glistening Veils of Ether

Veils of the cosmos twinkle with grace,
Draping the night in a silken embrace.
Infinite whispers on the wings of the stars,
Connect us to realms that are quietly ours.

Glistening pathways lead to the unknown,
In the midnight hush, we find seeds that are sown.
Ethereal dreams, glimmering bright,
Weaves through the darkness, igniting the night.

Every heartbeat echoes in this quiet expanse,
Timeless connections that beckon to dance.
With shimmers of hope, we rise and we fall,
Cascading through colors, we answer the call.

Awash in light, the cosmos unfurls,
Mingling our fates with the whispers of pearls.
Through glistening veils, our spirits take flight,
As we touch the infinite, embracing the light.

Beneath the Winter's Cloak

A tapestry woven with crystals of frost,
Lies gently hidden, too precious to toss.
Beneath this white cloak, a slumbering ground,
Dreams hibernate softly, their voices unbound.

The world whispers secrets in crystalline air,
Each flake that descends holds a tale to share.
Winter's embrace wraps around us with care,
Silencing echoes of burdens we bear.

Footsteps are muted on this shimmering white,
As shadows blend softly into the night.
With every soft breath, we savor the chill,
In the stillness, we find a peculiar thrill.

Branches adorned in a glistening sheen,
Draped in the silence, we ponder what's been.
Beneath the winter's cloak, we find a new phase,
A beauty that thrives in the cold's gentle gaze.

Together we linger in this frozen land,
Wrapped in the quiet, we take each other's hand.
As seasons will change, and warmth will ignite,
For now, let us cherish this tranquil twilight.

Milton Keynes UK
Ingram Content Group UK Ltd.
UKHW010229111224
452348UK00011B/618